Mexican Vegan Cookbook

Make Cooking at Home with 77 Vegan Mexican Recipes

By

Randy D. Turner

information is without contract or any type of guarantee assurance.

The trademarks that are used are without any consent, and the publication of the trademark is without permission or backing by the trademark owner. All trademarks and brands within this book are for clarifying purposes only and are owned by the owners themselves, not affiliated with this document.

Table of Contents

Introduction

Mexico is more stunning than the pure blue seas and tropical culture. Mexican food is famous for being delicious and exclusive. There is so much more to be found than burritos, chips, and guacamole in the Mexican food. You will note how essential and special cuisine is as you turn your attention through Mexico. All are entirely natural and delicious, abundant in color and taste, complete with seasonings that have a fair impact.

There is a lively background of authentic Mexican cuisine, and it is connected to the center of Mexican culture and ideals. To learn the Mexican roots, one of the best approaches is to learn its cuisine. Three major Mexican civilizations derive from many of the tastes, sights and sounds of traditional Mexican cuisine: Mayan, Aztec, and Spain.

The Mayans were nomadic, and the Mayan civilization is host to some of the most common foods. A staple was food made from maize, which is where corn tortillas are created. The Aztec Kingdom was in full force by the 1300s. Through their way of existence, the Aztecs would incorporate salt, pepper, and even cocoa. Spain conquered Mexico two hundred years later, and Mexican society was exposed to a whole bunch of modern foods. They imported dairy goods, cloves, and several spices and herbs.

The food system of Mexico is strongly rooted in meat-eating. They usually speak of beef tacos and meat dishes when people speak about Mexican cuisine. Although most Mexicans may have chuckled at people who do not consume meat a few years earlier but the vegetarian diet has now been embraced and incorporated into the cuisine of Mexico. Being so near to the United States, patterns, from entertainment to clothes, are inspired by American society, and food is no different. Now, residents of Mexico are also accepting a vegan diet.

The vegetarian aspect of Mexico is, however, less stated, but just as popular. Mexico is all about citrus fruits, legume forms, a wide variety of herbs, and a preference of fresh ingredients for cooking. It is a meat-focused nation, and there is no common vegetarianism, but thankfully in many dishes, there are vegetarian ingredients such as corn tortillas, rice, cheese, and vegetables.

In Mexico, the strongest choices for vegetarians are Enchilada, Quesadilla, Burritos, Meatless Lasagna, Pies, Vegan tacos, Tortillas and many more. These quick and inexpensive snacks can be found at street stalls. Most of these are focused on corn tortillas, and even if it is just cheese, you can normally get vegetarian variants and then liven them up with traditional toppings such as salsas. In this chapter, you will come to know about Vegetarian Mexican breakfast, lunch, snacks and dinner recipes.

Chapter 01: Vegetarian Mexican Breakfast Recipes

Flavorful breakfasts are common in Mexico. They are the start of your day. If you eat healthy and fresh at the beginning of your day, it is guaranteed that you would feel the same throughout the course of the day. Recipes in this chapter are for vegetarian persons.

❖ Chorizo and Eggs Ranchero

Time to cook: 25 minutes
Servings: 2

Ingredients:

- Tortillas (2 piece)
- Oil for frying
- ½ cup of beans (refried)
- ½ cup of chorizo
- 4 eggs (beaten)
- Half cup of salsa (medium)
- Half cup of cheese (shredded)

Instructions:

1. Firstly, set the oven to 425 degrees and let it warm. Moisturize the tortillas on both edges with oil. Bake for

12 minutes or until the surfaces turn brown. Let it cool for 5 minutes.

2. Roast the beans in the oven for 3-5 minutes.
3. Cook and scramble chorizo over a moderate flame in a broad skillet for 4-6 minutes or until it is cooked properly.
4. Clean the pan. Include eggs in it and scramble it. Fry it until browned. Heat salsa in the oven.
5. Assemble all the products over tortillas and serve it with cheese.

❖ Sopaipillas

Time to cook: 35 minutes
Servings: 12

Ingredients:

- 1 cup flour (all purpose)
- ½ teaspoon of baking powder
- Salt as per your taste
- ½ cup of warm water
- Oil
- ½ teaspoon of honey

Instructions:

1. Mix the rice, baking powder and salt in a wide dish. Tighten the paste until it resembles fine crumbs. Add water slowly and mix it properly.
2. Knead the dough for 2 minutes on a floured place. Cover and set it aside for 10 minutes.
3. Put the dough in the rectangle shape. Carve into 12 squares with a cutter.

4. Heat deep-oil fryer. Fry the sopaipillas on either hand for 1-2 minutes.
5. Drain on towels made of paper; stay wet. Serving with honey if needed

❖ Mexican Pancakes

Servings: 10
Time taken: 25 minutes

Ingredients:

- 2 cups of flour
- 1 cup of sugar and cinnamon
- Three Eggs (beaten)
- ½ cup of buttermilk
- ½ cup of sugar (powder)
- Ice-cream vanilla or honey for serving

Instructions:

1. In a cup, merge flour with sugar and mix them together. Eggs, milk and butter are whisked together.
2. Heat a skillet over moderate heat and cook a half cup of mixture for 3 minutes from both sides or until bubbles emerge on the top.
3. Serve with vanilla ice cream.

❖ Huevos Rancheros

Total time: 20 minutes
Servings: 4

Ingredients:

- Vegetable oil
- 4 tortillas (maize)
- 1 cup of beans (fried)
- One tablespoon of butter
- 4 eggs
- 1 cup of cheese (shredded)
- Half cup of salsa for serving

Instructions:

1. Melt butter over a moderate flame in a shallow skillet. Fry the tortillas for three minutes. Flush the grease from it by using paper towels.
2. In an oven, mix the refried beans and butter. Cook them in the oven until fully warmed. When the tortillas are cooked, fry in the skillet over simple eggs.
3. On the bowls, put the tortillas and spread a layer of beans on them.
4. Garnish with cheese, egg and salsa.

❖ Loaded Vegetables and Chorizo Egg Casserole

Time taken: 20 minutes
Servings: 4

Ingredients:

- Olive oil
- One onion (chopped)
- One cup of peas
- One potato (finely diced)
- Two chorizos (chopped)
- Two bell peppers (chopped)
- 1 cup of kale
- Salt and pepper as per your taste
- One tomato (chopped)
- 5 eggs
- Thyme and paprika
- 2 cups of cheese (shredded)
- Half cup of parmesan (shredded)

Instructions:

1. Warm the oil in a pan over a moderate flame. Add the onion and mushrooms and simmer until the mushrooms start browning.
2. Insert other vegetables, chorizo and spices in it and let them cook for around 10 minutes, stirring sometimes.
3. Place the vegetables in a 9-11 inch casserole dish and mix the tomatoes in it.
4. Mix the eggs with the paprika, cheese and thyme in a cup thoroughly.

5. In the casserole bowl, spill the eggs over the vegetables and blend until everything is well mixed.
6. Cover the casserole dish with anything and store it for one day at least.
7. Preheat the oven up to 270C and put the casserole in it and let it bake for 30 minutes. Serve it.

❖ Chiles Rellenos Soufflé

Time taken: 35 minutes

Servings: 6

Ingredients:

- Two cans of green chiles (cooked)
- 1 cup of cheese (sliced)
- 2 bell peppers (chopped)
- Four eggs
- ½ cup of milk
- Salt and pepper as per your taste
- Cilantro sprigs for serving

Instructions:

1. Preheat the oven to 220C. Sprinkle the oil over baking dish and place the chiles with slices of cheese in it. Sprinkle it with spices.
2. Mix the egg yolks and milk in a small bowl with a blender until it is well mixed. Also, add flour and salt to stir until smooth.
3. Whisk the egg whites in a wide bowl with the blender. Fold the yolk mixture softly into this. Mix the spoon uniformly over the stuffed chiles.

4. Bake for 35 minutes. Garnish with cilantro sprigs for each serving.

❖ Green Chile Quiche Squares

Time taken: 35 minutes
Servings: 3

Ingredients:

- 4 eggs
- Salt and pepper as per your taste
- One tablespoon sauce with cayenne pepper
- 3 cans of green chiles (diced)
- 2 cups of cheese (grated)
- 1 cup of cheddar cheese (shredded)

Instructions:

1. Firstly, preheated the oven up to 250C.
2. Grease the baking dish.
3. Add all ingredients in a cup. Blend well together.
4. In the baking dish, push the mixture down and bake for 40 minutes or until the center is firm
5. Enable to cool, then slice and serve in tiny squares.

❖ Vegetable Omelet Cups

Servings: 4
Total Time: 50 Minutes

Ingredients:

- ½ cup of tomatoes
- ½ cup of water
- Three eggs
- 1 tablespoon of coriander (minced)
- Butter (melted)
- Salt and pepper as per your taste
- 1 cup of cheese (shredded)
- One onion (chopped)
- Olive oil
- 2 tablespoons of olives (diced)

Instructions:

1. Combine the eggs, egg whites, cilantro, sugar, salt, pepper and water in a big cup.
2. Place a pan over moderate flame and sprinkle oil in it. Heat it for 2 minutes. Dump into the middle of the skillet around a half cup of the egg mixture—Cook for 3 minutes. Then, change the side and cook for 1 minute.
3. Remove and put it in a baking dish covered with cooking spray. Repeat with the remaining egg mixture and produce three more cups of an omelet.
4. Sprinkle cheese over it.
5. Preheat the oven to 350 degrees.

6. Simmer all chopped vegetables in the oil in a separate pan over a moderate flame until it turns soft. Spoon into cups of omelets.
7. Sprinkle the cheese over it.
8. Bake for 10-12 minutes or until it turns brown. Serve it warm.

❖ Flapjack

Time taken: 30 minutes
Servings: 3

Ingredients:

- Butter
- Brown Sugar
- Oats of porridge
- Golden syrup

Instructions:

1. Firstly, preheat the oven up to 180C.
2. Place a pan over a moderate flame. Put the butter, sugar, oats and syrup in it. Sauté it for 5 minutes.
3. Grease a baking dish with cooking oil.
4. Shift the flapjack mixture to the baking pan with oil.
5. Put for 30 minutes in the preheated oven or until the sides tend to turn brown.
6. Cut them into slices and serve.

❖ Cheese Enchiladas

Time: 35 minutes
Servings: 5

Ingredients:

- 1 cup of cheddar cheese (shredded)
- 5 tortillas (maize)
- Oil
- One onion (chopped)
- Enchilada salsa (cooked)
- Guacamole
- Sour milk

Instructions:

1. Firstly, preheat the oven up to 250C. Fry tortillas in the frying oil in a separate pan.
2. Soak the tortillas in spicy enchilada sauce to coat them after you do this. Now, place the tortillas on a plate for a minute to cool off.
3. Put grated cheese over it then sprinkle the middle of one tortilla with some onion and fold it.
4. Lightly bake it in the oven.
5. Serve it.

❖ Mexican Filed Omelet

Servings: 8
Time needed: 40 minutes

Ingredients:

- One avocado
- Three limes
- Cilantro
- Yoghurt
- Olive oil
- One onion (chopped)
- 1 carrot (chopped)
- Salt and pepper as per your taste
- Eight eggs
- 1 cup of cheese (shredded)

Instructions:

1. In a mixer, squeeze the avocado flesh. Rip the cilantro stalks, apply the yoghurt and a splash of oil and blend it well. Add seasoning and lime in it.
2. Chop all the other ingredients.
3. Mix vegetables, blended mixture, cheese and eggs together.
4. Put oil in the pan over a moderate heat. Add quarter of egg mixture in it. Gently cook the omelet for 3 minutes.
5. Serve it.

❖ Mexican Style Sandwich

Time taken: 25 minutes
Servings: 2

Ingredients:

- Four white bread slices
- Half cup of beans (refried)
- Four tablespoons of corn (cooked)
- Cheese (shredded)
- Two chili peppers (chopped)

Instructions:

1. Place a sheet of refried beans over each piece of bread.
2. Assemble all other ingredients over that layer.
3. In a sandwich maker, grill the sandwiches for 5 minutes or until the cheese starts to melt.

❖ Apple Pie Baked French Toast

Servings: 10
Time to cook: 50 minutes

Ingredients:

- 20 pieces of bread
- Apple pie sauce
- Eight Eggs (beaten)
- 2 cups of milk
- Vanilla extract (1 teaspoon)
- Cinnamon (1 teaspoon)

For Topping:

- Half cup of brown sugar
- Half cup of butter

Instructions:

1. Assemble ten bread slices in a greased baking dish. Spread over the filling of the pie.
2. Mix all other ingredients thoroughly. Pour over the bread.
3. Bake for 35-40 minutes in a preheated oven up to 250C.
4. Serve it.

❖ Spinach and Mushroom Egg Muffins

Servings: 6
Time taken: 35 minutes

Ingredients:

- Six Eggs
- Half cup of milk
- One teaspoon of garlic (powdered)
- Salt and pepper as per your taste
- 2 cups of spinach (chopped)
- 6 ounce of mushrooms (diced)

Instructions:

1. Firstly, preheat the furnace to 350F.
2. Add the eggs, cream and all seasonings to a wide mixing dish. Properly whisk together.

3. Cut the mushrooms and spinach and whisk them into the mixture.
4. Put a full spoon of this mixture in a greased muffin tins.
5. Bake it all for 30 minutes. Serve it.

❖ Fried Egg Toast

Servings: 4
Period Required: 25 minutes

Ingredients:

- Four sandwich bread slices
- Olive oil
- Four eggs
- 1 tomato (chopped)
- Spices as per your taste
- 2 cups of parmesan cheese (shredded)

Instructions:

1. Make a void in the middle of each bread slice using a cutter. Warm oil over moderate to high heat in a skillet. Cook for approximately 2 minutes.
2. Place a mixture of eggs and other ingredients in that void. Decrease the heat to low. Put a lid over a skillet and cook for 3 to 4 minutes.
3. Serve it.

❖ Aztec Baked Eggs

Servings: 6
Time taken: 35 minutes

Ingredients:

- Butter
- Six Eggs
- Pepper and salt, to taste
- Other ingredients include chopped ham, chopped green onions and shredded cheese.

Instructions:

1. Firstly, preheat the furnace to 250C.
2. Grease muffin tins with oil.
3. Put one egg in each muffin tin. Insert ingredients of your choosing.
4. Bake for 13 minutes. Immediately serve.

❖ Eggs with Fried Tortillas

Servings: 2
Period required: 30 minutes

Ingredients:

- Two eggs
- 2 tortillas
- One onion and tomato (chopped)
- Coriander
- Olive oil as per your need

- Salt and pepper as per your taste

Instructions:

1. In a skillet, heat the oil, insert chopped vegetables and sauté for around 5 minutes or until tender.
2. Add all the spices in it and let it simmer for 2 minutes.
3. Put the beaten eggs into the pan and cook for 4-5 minutes over a mild fire, stirring until the eggs are lightly scrambled.
4. Warm the tortillas. Split the tortillas between the eggs and serve.

❖ Mexican Style Corn

Total time: 35 minutes
Servings: 4

Ingredients:

- Four ears of corn
- ½ cup of mayonnaise
- ½ cup of parmesan cheese (shredded)
- Chili, pepper and salt as per your taste

Instructions:

1. Boil ears of corn in a pan filled with water over moderate heat for 25 minutes or until it turn soft.
2. Pour mayonnaise all over the kernels. Sprinkle the Parmesan cheese evenly around the ear and chili powder.
3. Repeat with the leftover corn ears.

❖ Churro Doughnuts

Servings: 12
Time taken: 45 minutes

Ingredients:

- Half cup of sugar (melted)
- 1 teaspoon of vanilla essence
- Three Eggs
- Salt (pinch)
- Cinnamon (half teaspoon)
- 2 cups of flour
- One teaspoon of baking powder
- One cup of milk

Instructions:

1. Whisk in the butter until foamy. Add sugar and vanilla extract steadily and beat them to produce a smooth mixture.
2. Combine the baking powder and the rice, cinnamon and nutmeg. To the creamed mixture, apply the flour mixture alternately with the milk.
3. Spoon the doughnut batter into a non-stick baking tin. Put in the 350 F preheated oven and bake for 15 minutes or until the toothpick inserted into the doughnut comes out clean.
4. Garnish it with any topping.

❖ Sweet Potato Hash

Serving: 1
Period Required: 40 minutes.

Ingredients:

- One sweet potato (diced)
- Olive oil
- 1 onion (diced)
- 1 teaspoon of cumin
- Chili powder, salt and pepper as per your need
- ½ teaspoon of garlic
- One egg
- 3 tablespoons of mozzarella cheese (shredded)

Instructions:

1. Cook your finely sliced sweet potato for about 10-15 minutes.
2. In a pan, heat up the olive oil and add your onions, red pepper, sweet potato and spices in it.
3. Keep frying until the exterior of the sweet potato becomes crispy.
4. Spread it all in the pan equally and smash an egg in the middle. Cook until the egg white is almost cooked.
5. Sprinkle shredded mozzarella over it and put under the skillet until it is melted.
6. Serve it with anything.

Chapter 02: Vegetarian Mexican Lunch Recipes

The main meals of a day are usually taken for lunch. We typically have light breakfast and dinner but have a heavy lunch. A list of such recipes has been shared in this chapter which can be served for lunch. These lunch recipes are specifically Vegetarian Mexican Lunch recipes. Let us just dig into it.

❖ Mexican Black Beans and Rice

Servings: 4
Time took: 35 minutes

Ingredients:

- Oil as per you required
- One small onion (chopped)
- Clove of garlic (minced)
- ½ tablespoon of cumin
- 1 tablespoon of tomato (puree)
- Water
- Salt and pepper as per your taste
- Grain rice (250g)
- One tablespoon of coriander
- Beans (rinsed and washed)

Instructions:

1. Preheat oil in a pan over moderate flame. For 5 minutes, sauté the onion and garlic or until it turns tender.

2. Add all other ingredients, spices and the rice in it and let it cook for 10 minutes. Put a lid over a pan and lower the temperature and cook it until the rice is tender and the water has been diluted.
3. Add black beans in it and let it cook until it is fully cooked.
4. Serve it.

❖ Black Bean Lasagna

Servings: 10
Time required: 35 minutes

Ingredients:

- One onion (chopped)
- One green pepper (chopped)
- Oil
- 4 to 6 cloves of garlic (minced)
- 1 can of tomato (puree)
- Salt, pepper and chili as per your taste
- One can black beans (rinsed)
- 1 cup of pinto beans (rinsed)
- Three cups of cheese (shredded)
- One egg (beaten)
- Parsley
- Four tortillas (halved)

Instructions:

1. Put a pan with oil over a moderate flame. Add onion, garlic, tomatoes and spices in it and let it simmer for 5-8 minutes.
2. Add beans in it and let it cook for another 10 minutes.
3. Grease a baking a dish. Put half of the mixture of bean in it. Spread it thoroughly over it.
4. Mix cheese, egg white and jalapeno in the separate bowl and put this mixture in a baking dish. Make layers like this.
5. Bake in a preheated oven at 350C for 25 minutes.

6. Let it cool first, then serve it.

❖ Jicama Tortillas

Servings: 4
Period required: 15 minutes

Ingredients:

- One medium Jicama
- Olive Oil
- Salt and pepper as per your need
- Paprika

Instructions:

1. Firstly, peel and slice jicama into tortillas.
2. Drizzle oil, salt and paprika over it.
3. Heat the tortillas on either side for about a minute, before they are soft and slightly tender.
4. Serve them with anything of your liking.

❖ Black Bean & Quinoa Enchilada

Servings: 5
Total time: 30 minutes

Ingredients:

- 1 cup of quinoa (rinsed and washed)
- One tin of black beans (rinsed and washed)
- One sweet potato (peeled and sliced)

- 2 cups of maize
- 1 cup of tomatoes (diced)
- Taco seasoning
- One cup of enchilada sauce
- Water
- 2 cups of spinach (chopped)
- ½ cup of Mexican cheese blend

Instructions:

1. Mix the cleaned all ingredients, spices and 1/2 cup of water in a moderate pan.
2. Put a lid over it and let it cook until the quinoa turns soft.
3. Simmer in the cheese and spinach.
4. Serve it with any of topping.

❖ Caramelized Onion & Jalapeno Quesadilla

Time required: 35 minutes.
Servings: 10

Ingredients:

- Olive oil
- One big onion (chopped)
- 1 tablespoon of balsamic vinegar
- One teaspoon of sugar
- Ten tortillas
- 1 cup of fontina cheese (shredded)
- 1 cup of goat cheese (shredded)

Instructions:

1. Firstly you have to caramelized onion for this, heat olive oil and onions in a pan. Cook until it turns soft.
2. Add spices and sugar in it and let it simmer for 4 minutes.
3. Grease a baking dish and place three tortillas and put cheese and caramelized onions over it. Cover it with tortillas. Brush the top of tortillas with olive oil.
4. Put the dish in a preheated oven at 250C for 10 minutes or until the tortillas turn brown.
5. Serve it.

❖ Santa Fe Veggie Quesadilla

Servings: 4
Period Required: 10 minutes

Ingredients:

- 1 tortilla
- 1 cup of cheese (shredded)
- Half cup of corn (drained)
- Half cup of red bell pepper (chopped)
- Half cup of black beans (rinsed and washed)
- One onion (chopped)

Instructions:

1. Over moderate flame, cook a finely oiled medium pan. To provide an equal layer of oil on all sides, put the tortilla in the pan and turn it again.
2. Enable 3 minutes to heat the tortilla on the one hand.

3. Layer the cheese mixture uniformly, starting at the middle of the tortilla, until the whole layer of the tortilla is coated. Place the vegetables on top of the cheese.
4. Cut tortilla and serve it warm.

❖ Bean Burrito

Servings: 8
Time required: 60 minutes

Ingredients:

- 1 cup of rice
- Olive oil
- Two onions (chopped)
- Four cloves of garlic (minced)
- Half tablespoon of cumin
- Salt and pepper as per your taste
- Two tablespoons of paste of tomato
- Two cans of pinto beans (washed and rinsed)
- One cup of corn
- Five scallions (sliced)
- Eight tortillas
- 2 cups of cheese (shredded)
- Salsa for topping

Instructions:

1. Firstly, cook rice and set it aside.
2. In a broad skillet, warm oil over moderate flame. Add all spices, onion, garlic and tomatoes in it.

3. Cook, stirring regularly, for 12 minutes or until it turns golden.
4. Include the beans and one cup of water. Put a lid over the pan and boil it for 10 to 12 minutes or until thickened.
5. After this, add scallions and corn in it and let t cook for 5 minutes.
6. Prepare tortillas and fill it with bean mixture and cheese.
7. Assemble all the prepare ingredient together and place it in the baking dish and let it bake until the tortillas turn brown.
8. Serve it with salsa or any other topping.

❖ Zucchini Enchiladas

Period Required: 30 minutes
Servings: 5

Ingredients:

- Olive oil
- One onion (chopped)
- Two tablespoons of garlic (minced)
- One teaspoon of cumin
- Salt, pepper and chili as per your taste
- 1 cup of sauce enchilada
- Four zucchini (halved)
- 2 cups of cheddar cheese (shredded)

Instructions:

1. Firstly, preheat the oven to 250C. Warm the oil in a wide pan over moderate flame.

2. Add the onion, cumin, spices and garlic in it and let it simmer for 5-10 minutes or until it turns tender.
3. Insert 1 cup of enchilada sauce and let it cook for a while.
4. Peel thin slices of zucchini. Cover with a spoonful of cooked mixture and set out three slices, somewhat intertwined.
5. Wrap up and move to a tray for baking. Repeat with the mixture of remaining zucchini and prepared mixture.
6. Put the cheese over it.
7. Bake for 20 minutes, before the cheese, is melted and the enchiladas are cooked.
8. Serve it with sour cream or any other topping of your liking.

❖ Mushroom and Onion Tacos

Servings: 4
Period Required: 30 minutes

Ingredients:

- One tablespoon oil
- One onion (sliced)
- Three mushrooms (chopped properly)
- Two teaspoons taco seasoning
- Water
- Tortillas
- Half cup of fresco cheese (shredded)

Instruction:

1. Melt butter over mid to low flame in a pan. Cook the onion and mushrooms in it and let it cook for 7 minutes or until it turns soft.
2. Lower the heat and add seasonings, water and spices in it. Cook for about 5 minutes or before it consumes water.
3. Fill tortillas with the cooked mixture and put cheese over it.
4. Serve it.

❖ Veggie Pizzadillas

Servings: 4
Period Required: 30 minutes

Ingredients:

- Eight tortillas
- 1 cup of tomato pasta sauce
- 1 cup of mozzarella (shredded)
- Dried oregano
- Salt and pepper as per your taste
- Sliced vegetables of your liking
- Olive oil

Instructions:

1. Combine the sauce, cheese and spices in a bowl and mix it thoroughly.
2. Place over each tortilla, then put sliced vegetables over it.
3. Put oil and oregano in a pan and let it get warm for 3 minutes. Rub it over the pizza Dallas on either side.
4. Fry them on either side until they are golden and crisp.

5. Cut into wedges and serve in slices.

❖ Mexican Meatless Lasagna

Servings: 5
Period Taken: Fifty Minutes

Ingredients:

- 1 cup of corns
- Onion, tomatoes and chilies (chopped)
- Half cup of black beans (rinsed)
- Six tortillas
- 2 tablespoons of taco seasoning
- 1 cup red and green bell pepper (sliced)
- 1 cup of beans (refried)
- 1 cup sauce of enchilada
- 1 cup of cheddar cheese (shredded)

Instructions:

1. Firstly, preheat the oven to 350°C. Grease a baking dish and put it aside.
2. Mix the corn, tomatoes and chiles in a moderate dish. Place a broad pan over moderate flame.
3. Add wedges of tortillas, taco seasoning and soy sauce in it and let it cook for 4 minutes. Put it aside. Add remaining vegetable spices in a pan and let it cook for 10 minutes or until it turns tender.
4. In the baking tray, assemble all ingredients together and put cheese over it. You have to assemble it in layers.
5. Bake for about 20 minutes or until it turns brown.

❖ Bean Pie

Servings: 5
Time required: 60 minutes

Ingredients:

- Piecrusts
- Two eggs
- 1 cup of beans
- Evaporated milk
- Half cup of sugar
- Half tablespoon of spice pumpkin pie
- Salt as per your taste
- Cream whipped for topping

Instructions:

1. Firstly, preheat the oven to 270C. Place the piecrust into a baking pie dish.
2. In a cup, whisk together all other ingredients. Pour in the piecrust mixture.
3. Bake it for 50 minutes in a preheated oven. Let it cool for a while.
4. Top it with whipped cream and serve it.

❖ Vegan Tacos

Servings: 2
Time required: 20 minutes

Ingredients:

- 2 cups of beans
- 1 cup of tomato sauce
- 1 tablespoon of cumin
- One avocado (diced)
- Half cup of corn
- Eight shells of taco

Instructions:

1. Put a broad pan over moderate flame and cook beans, tomatoes and spices in it for 10 minutes.
2. Insert the bean mixture in the tacos and top it with toppings of your liking. Serve it with garnishing.

❖ Red Beans and Rice Burritos

Servings: 6
Time required: 35 minutes

Ingredients:

- Water
- 1 cup of brown rice
- 1 Onion and green pepper (chopped)
- Olive oil
- 1 teaspoon of garlic (minced)
- Salt and chili as per your taste
- One can of black beans (rinsed)
- Eight tortillas
- Salsa

Instructions:

1. Put a pan filled with water, rice and salt over moderate heat. Let it boil for a while until it is cooked.
2. Add oil, all other spices, onions, garlic and beans in another pan and let it cook for 10 minutes or until the mixture turn soft.
3. Add boiled rice in it and let it simmer for 4 minutes.
4. Fill each tortilla with the above prepared and put cheese and salsa over it.
5. Serve it.

❖ Chard Tacos

Time required: 20 minutes
Servings: 3

Ingredients:

- Olive oil
- One big onion (chopped)
- 2 teaspoons of garlic (minced)
- Water
- One bunch of Swiss chard (chopped)
- Salt and pepper as per your taste
- 8 tortillas
- 1 cup of fresco cheese (shredded)
- Salsa

Instructions:

1. Put a pan over a medium flame. Add oil, onions, garlic and all other spices in it. Let it cook until onion turns soft.
2. Add other ingredients in it. Put a lid over the pan. Simmer it for 8 minutes.
3. Set it aside.
4. Heat the tortillas in another heated pan on either side for roughly 1 minute. Cover the chard with the cooked tortillas and finish with the salsa or cheese.

❖ Fried Avocado Tacos

Time required: 20 minutes
Servings: 7

Ingredients:

- Half cup of wheat
- 2 Eggs
- 1 cup of breadcrumbs
- Two avocados (sliced)
- Oil
- Salt and pepper as per your taste
- 2 cups of cabbage (chopped)
- 1 cup of cheese (shredded)
- Salsa
- 8 Tortillas

Instructions:

1. In three different cups, put the rice, eggs, and breadcrumbs separately. Submerge the rims of the avocado in rice.
2. Cover with egg, then breadcrumbs.
3. In deep pan, heat oil over moderate flame. Fry the avocado, around 1 to 2 minutes per foot, until golden brown.
4. Segregate the avocado slices equally between the tortillas to build the tacos. Add cabbage, cheese and other seasonings on the top of it.

❖ Vegan Mexican Rice

Servings: 5
Period Required: 40 minutes

Ingredients:

- 2 cups of rice
- 1 cup of black beans
- Half cup of sweet corn
- One onion (chopped)
- One red bell pepper (sliced)
- Half teaspoon of sliced jalapeno
- Half teaspoon of garlic powder
- One cube of bouillon
- One tablespoon of tomato puree
- Lime zest
- Oil
- Water
- Salt as per you taste

Instructions:

1. Add oil, onion, spices, bell pepper, garlic, tomato paste and a cube of bouillon in a pan and put it over moderate flame. Let it cook for 5-10 minutes.
2. Then, add beans in it and let it cook until it is cooked. Add rice, water, spices in it and put a lid over it. Let it boil until the water is absorbed.
3. Squeeze the juice with fresh lime and serve it.

❖ Vegan Chickpea and Vegetable Tacos

Servings: 4
Time required: 15 minutes.

Ingredients:

- 2 cans of chickpeas (rinsed)
- Half cup of water
- 1 tablespoon of taco seasoning
- Eight shells of taco

Instructions:

1. Add the chickpeas, taco spices and water over a moderate flame in a skillet. Cook and mix for 5 to 7 minutes until fully cooked.
2. Mash the mixture of chickpeas to crush.
3. Divide the chickpea filling between the taco shells equally.

❖ Vegetarian Portabella Mushroom Enchilada

Servings: 5
Time took: 90 minutes

Ingredients:

- One tablespoon of vinegar
- One teaspoon of sugar
- Five tablespoons of fresh lime juice
- One big onion (chopped)
- One chipotle Chile
- Two tablespoon of heavy cream
- Salt and pepper as per your taste
- Vegetable oil
- Three big mushrooms (chopped)
- One clove of garlic (minced)
- 12 tortillas
- 6 ounces of fresh cheese (shredded)
- 1 cup of cheddar (shredded)

Instructions:

1. Firstly, preheat the oven to 250C.
2. Mix sugar, lime zest and syrup in a separate bowl.
3. Add Chile, half cup of milk, salt and cream in a blender. Blend it well. Set it aside.
4. Put pan with oil over moderate flame.
5. Add mushrooms, Chile, garlic, and onion in it. Fry them until mushrooms turn tender. Season it with spices.
6. In the meantime, heat tortillas in the microwave.
7. Grease baking dish with oil. Spread the cream sauce evenly in the baking dish.

8. Cover tortillas with cream sauce thoroughly. Put it in the baking dish.
9. Assemble all other ingredients over the tortillas.
10. Spoon the leftover sauce over the enchiladas, ensuring sure that the sauce is fully coated. Cover with cheddar.
11. Bake enchiladas for 35 minutes until the sides of the tortillas turn brown.
12. Serve it warm.

Chapter 03: Vegetarian Mexican Snacks Recipes

Whenever you are mild hungry and do not want to eat anything heavy, then snacks are the best option available to you. Snacks are also easy to make, and you can eat them at any-time. In this chapter, you will come to know about recipes of Vegetarian Mexican snacks that can be prepared easily by following given instructions.

❖ Quick Microwave Nachos

Serving: 1
Total time: 15 minutes

Ingredients:

- Tortilla chips (1 cup)
- Taco sauce (¼ cup)
- Mexican shredded cheese (1 cup)

Instructions:

1. Assemble the tortilla chips in any plate that is microwaveable.
2. Cover with tacos spices and cheese in a uniform way.
3. Let it microwave for 3 minutes uncovered. Put a cover on it and let it heat for one more minute or until cheese is completely melted.
4. Garnish it with preferred toppings and serve.

❖ Cheese and Bell Pepper Quesadillas

Servings: 20
Period Taken: Fifty minutes
Ingredients:

- One green bell pepper (washed and sliced)
- One red bell pepper (sliced)
- One yellow bell pepper (sliced)
- One onion (finely chopped)
- One tablespoon of garlic powder
- Pepper, chilies and salt as per your taste
- Butter
- ¼ tablespoon of cumin
- 1 cup of cream cheese (whisked)
- ½ cup of cheddar cheese (shredded)
- Tortillas
- Sour cream and salsa for topping

Instructions:

1. Put a pan with butter over moderate flame and let the butter melts.
2. Add bell peppers, garlic powder, chopped onions and cumin in it.
3. Let it cook for 3-4 minutes and then add spices in it. Let it simmer for 2 minutes.
4. Drain extra oil from the mixture and set it aside.
5. Mix the chilies, cream cheese and one teaspoon of fresh garlic together in a separate bowl. Then, add the cheddar cheese and mix it thoroughly.
6. Spread each tortilla with between 4 teaspoons of the cheese mixture.

7. Top it with cooked mixture and then roll tortillas. Put the butter over the tortilla thinly and dust it with cumin or any other spices. Put the tortilla slices on a thinly greased baking dish.
8. Heat the oven at 400 degrees.
9. Bake for around 15 minutes or until tortillas turns brown.
10. Cut tortillas into slices. Garnish it with salsa or any other topping of your liking and serve.

❖ Nachos with Vegan Cheese Sauce

Servings: 3
Time took: 30 minutes

Ingredients:

- Cashew casserole (1 cup)
- Olive oil
- Half of the onion (finely chopped)
- Two cloves of garlic (minced)
- Chilies, pepper and salt as per your taste
- Half cup of milk
- One tablespoon of yeast
- One tablespoon of lime zest
- Mustard (optional)
- Water
- Tortilla chips
- 1 cup of black beans (rinsed and drained)
- Salsa
- Guacamole

Instructions:

1. Put the cashews in a shallow pan and water in it at room temperature. Let it simmer for minimum one hour to two hours. Then, drain water from it.
2. Over moderate flame, heat the oil in a pan. Add the oil, accompanied by the onion. Let it cook for a few minutes and continue stirring it.
3. Add the garlic and all spices in it. Stir and let it cook for 4-5 minutes. After cooking, set it aside.
4. To a mixer, put soaked cashews, a mixture of onion, milk, yeast, lime zest, mustard, salt and pepper as per your taste. Put a lid on it and blend it well. Add ¼ cup of water in it to gain uniform consistency.
5. In a saucepan, put the blended sauce and cook over a moderate flame, stir continuously. It should not be thickened.
6. Start piling up half of the chips on plates, put the cooked sauce over it, and sprinkle with cheese sauce and salsa.
7. Garnish it with guacamole. Serve it.

❖ Mango Salsa

Servings: 5
Time took: 10 minutes

Ingredients:

- One mango (peeled and sliced)
- Half cup of cucumber
- One teaspoon jalapeno
- ½ cup onion (finely sliced)

- Lime zest
- Coriander leaves
- Pepper and salt as per your taste

Instructions:

1. Mix all the ingredients, spices and lime juice together and blend it properly with the help of a blender.
2. Taste it, if you want to add more salt and pepper, you can add it. Serve it.

❖ Bread Rolls

Servings: 16
Time took: 3 hours

Ingredients:

- 2 cups of warm water
- Two teaspoons of yeast
- One tablespoon of sugar
- Vegetable oil
- Salt and pepper as per your taste
- 4 cups of flour

Instructions:

1. Place a wide bowl. Mix the water, sugar, and yeast together in it.
2. Set it aside for around 12 minutes or until it turns creamy. Put the oil, salt, and flour to the above mixture.
3. Mix the mixture together and slowly add more flour to it as per your need and knead the mixture to form a dough.
4. Roll out on a gentle sheet pan and knead for around 5 minutes until it is smooth and flexible. Position the

dough in the tub and gently sprinkle oil over it and cover it with a lid.

5. Set it aside for 1 hour and let it rise until it turns twice in size.
6. Dampen the dough, then on a floured board, turn it out. Cut the dough into 16 equal parts and mould into balls that are circular. Place them apart on thinly lubricated baking sheets. Top the rolls with a moist cloth and let them put aside for around 40 minutes before they have risen in size.
7. In the meanwhile, preheat the oven up to 200C.
8. Put a baking dish in an oven.
9. Let it bake for 25 minutes or until it turns golden brown.

❖ Huevos Diablos

Period Required: 40 minutes
Servings: 6

Ingredients:

- Olive oil
- One onion (chopped)
- One tablespoon of garlic
- 1 cup of tomatoes (chopped)
- One teaspoon of sauce from Worcestershire
- ¾ cup of Parmesan cheese (shredded)
- Six eggs
- Butter
- Six tortillas (corn)

Instructions:

1. Warm olive oil over a moderate flame in a large frying pan. Fry, the onion for around 6 minutes or until it, turns smooth, transparent, and brown. Stir in the garlic and let it simmer for 1 minute.
2. Stir in the spices, tomato sauce and other sauce.
3. Carry it to a simmer at low flame and cook for around 10 minutes.
4. In the meanwhile, the oven should be preheated 175C.
5. Put a bowl and mix in tomato sauce with shredded Parmesan cheese.
6. In 6 tiny oven-safe cups that greased with oil, put a mixture of sauce in it. On top of each one, split one egg and sprinkle with butter. Toss with the Parmesan cheese.
7. Bake it for 25 minutes in the oven, uncovered, or until the egg whites are firm, but the yolks are still fluffy.
8. Serve it with tortillas or bread.

❖ Grilled Pepper Popper

Servings: 6
Time took: 35 minutes

Ingredients:

- ¼ cup of cream (whisked)
- 16 sweet peppers
- 1 cup of Mexican cheese (shredded)
- One tomato (finely chopped)
- ½ cup of onion (finely chopped)
- Two tablespoons of cilantro
- Salt and pepper as per your taste

Instructions:

1. Put a spoon of sour cream into a bag in the freezer and let it cool for a while.
2. In the meanwhile, preheat the grill to a moderate temperature.
3. Rinse or wash the peppers and cut it into lengthwise in halves. You also have to remove their seeds.
4. Blend the cheese, onions, cabbage, cilantro and spices together in a shallow dish.
5. Fill the pepper halves equally with the mixture of cheese and press it so that it can fill it with leaving any hollows.
6. Put it into a baking dish and let it bake from the above side.
7. Cook until the hems are scorched and mildly burnt for around 5 minutes.
8. Shift the peppers to the plate with the help of a large spatula.
9. Cut off the sour cream in the bag and pour over the hot peppers equally.
10. Immediately serve.

❖ Fried Jalapenos

Servings: 6
Time took: 20 minutes

Ingredients:

- Flour (1 cup)
- Salt, chilies and pepper as per your taste
- Two eggs
- Oil
- 2 cups of jalapeno peppers (chopped)

Instructions:

1. In a cup, blend together the flour, salt, spices, garlic powder, and eggs.
2. Add the oil in a deep fryer and let it heat to 180C.
3. In the above-mixed batter, insert the cut jalapenos. Place the deep fryer with the battered jalapenos.
4. When they rise to the top of the liquid, the jalapenos are completely fried. They are meant to be lightly browned and crispy.

❖ Grilled Corn

Time took: 50 minutes
Servings: 6

Ingredients:

- Eight ears of corn
- Salt and pepper as per your taste

For BBQ butter:

- One tablespoon of canola oil
- Half red onion (chopped)
- One tablespoon of garlic powder
- One tablespoon of paprika
- One teaspoon of cumin seeds (roasted)
- Chilies, salt and pepper as per your taste
- Half cup of water
- Butter

Instructions:

1. Firstly, heat the grill up to medium temperature or flame.
2. Take the outer hollows of corns to the neck. Completely remove it by hand from each ear of grain.
3. Cover the husks back in order and place the maize ears for 15 minutes in a wide bowl of cold water with salt.
4. Drain the water from maize and let it dry for a while. Set up the corn on the grill, close the cover of the grill and let it cook for 15 minutes, rotating every 5 minutes or until its corn turn tender.
5. Using the BBQ butter, spread over the corn when served.
6. Preheat over a moderate flame in a wide pan. Insert the onion and cook for 2 or 3 minutes until it is tender. Add

all other ingredients in it and let it cook for a while. Add water and spices in it and let it boil for 5 minutes or until the mixture thickens. Set it aside and let it cool for a while.

7. In a food processor, put the butter and above mixture in it. Grind it well until a uniform consistency is created.
8. Put it aside for 30 minutes before using it further.

❖ Spicy Refried Beans

Servings: 2
The period required: 35 minutes

Ingredients:

- One onion (chopped)
- One pepper jalapeno (chopped)
- One tablespoon of garlic powder
- Oil
- 1 cup of beans (refried)
- Water
- Pepper and salt as per your taste
- ½ teaspoon of cumin field

Instructions:

1. Put a medium-size deep-pan above a medium flame.
2. Place beans and shredded Monterey Jack cheese in it. Add water in it that should be around 2 inches.
3. Carry the beans to a simmer. After some time, remove it from the flame and set it aside.

4. Meanwhile, the chiles are washed and dried. Cover them with oil and put on a plain baking pan under the oven for around 10 minutes, rotating once in a while. When the skin turns blackish and blistered, remove it from the oven.
5. Chop the garlic and chiles. Set them aside
6. Remove the beans mixture from the bowl after 1 hour, and put them in the slow cooker. To be around 1 inch above the beans, cover with adequate water. Include the diced chiles, ginger, onions and ground garlic.
7. Cook for 8 hours on high temperature.
8. You can spice them and consume them as they are and you can refry them when the beans are cooked.

❖ Chipotle Lime Corn Cobs

Servings: 6
Time took: 40 minutes

Ingredients:

- Six ears of sweet corn
- Mayonnaise
- One chipotle pepper sauce
- One tablespoon of coriander
- One tablespoon of lime zest
- ½ cup of Asiago cheese (shredded)

Instructions:

1. Start peeling the corn husks gently.
2. Maize is rewrapped in husks and tied with kitchen cord. In a large pan, put the cold water along with salt. Let it soak for 30 minutes.

3. Grill the corn, and cover for 25 minutes or until it turns tender after turning sometimes.
4. Place the remaining ingredients in a shallow dish. Mix them thoroughly. Over each sweet corn, add one tablespoon of this mixture on top.
5. Sprinkle with cheese and some lime zest. Just serve it.

❖ Creamy Pumpkin Soup

Servings: 5

Time took: 50 minutes

Ingredients:

- Two tablespoons of butter
- Two teaspoons of sugar
- Four bread slices

For the soup:

- 1 cup onion (chopped)
- Sugar
- 2 cups of water
- Pumpkin puree
- Salt and pepper as per your taste
- ¼ tablespoon of ginger powder
- 1 cup of milk (whipped)

Instructions:

1. Firstly, preheat the oven to 200 degrees C.
2. Mix the melted butter, sugar and cinnamon to produce coleslaw.
3. Range the butter mixture equally over one side of each piece of bread. Put bread on a greased baking dish, buttered side up.

4. Bake it for 5 minutes or just until the bread is crisp. Start cutting each bread slice into eight little triangles.
5. Simmer the onion in a medium saucepan with butter until it turns soft.
6. Add water in it. Put a lid over it and reduce the flame to low and simmer for 15 minutes. Bring it to a boil.
7. Move the above mixture into the blender. Blend it until it turns smooth.
8. Shift the mixture back to the skillet.
9. Add the water, pumpkin, salt, ground cinnamon, ground ginger and ground pepper to the pan. Mix it well. Carry it to a boil. Put a lid over it and reduce the flame. Let it simmer, stirring periodically, for ten more minutes.
10. Stir in the cream and heat up. Serve it.

❖ Grilled Guacamole

Servings: 4
Time took: 20 minutes

Ingredients:

- Olive Oil
- Four avocados (peeled)
- Lime zest (1 tablespoon)
- Salt and pepper as per your taste
- ¼ onion (finely chopped)

Instructions:

1. Initially, preheat barbecue grill on low flame. Grease it well.

2. Peel and cut an avocado in halves. Grease half of each avocado gently with oil.
3. Set the cut-side avocados down on the barbecue. Cover and cook, around 5 minutes per hand, until warmed through and grill marks emerge.
4. To a wide cup, move the avocados and let them cool slightly. With a fork, break. Sprinkle in the lime zest and the spices to the seasoning.
5. Serve with chips instantly.

❖ Mexican Bread Tartlets

Servings: 6
Time took: 35 minutes

Ingredients:

- Six bread slices
- 1 cup of cheese (shredded)
- One potato (baked and sliced)
- One onion (chopped)
- One tomato (finely chopped)
- Six olives (pitted)
- Salt, pepper and chili as per your taste
- Half teaspoon of basil and oregano powder
- Olive oil

Instructions:

1. Trim the sides of bread slices. Then, place these slices in greased muffin tins.
2. Sprinkle some oil over it.

3. Bake at 200C for 10-12 minutes in a preheated oven until the bread is crisp and browned.
4. Meanwhile, chop all the vegetables.
5. Remove the tray from oven and place the apples, tomatoes and onions in it.
6. Also, sprinkle all spices and shredded cheese over it.
7. Bake in the oven for 10 minutes or until cheese gets brown.
8. Serve any garnishing of your liking.

❖ Mexican French Fries

Servings: 2
Period Required: 30 minutes
Ingredients:

- Sour cream
- Fries
- Mexican cheese dip
- Onion (chopped)
- Taco seasoning

Instructions:

1. Firstly, preheat the deep fryer. Fry fries in it for 15 minutes or until it turns golden brown.
2. Assemble fries and all other ingredients in a plate and heat it in a microwave for 3 minutes or until cheese melts.

❖ Crispy Fried Cauliflower

Servings: 4
Time took: 35 minutes

Ingredients:

- One cauliflower (washed and chopped)
- Salt and pepper as per your taste
- One teaspoon of onion powder, oregano, paprika, and garlic powder
- Flour (2 cups)
- Two tablespoons of cornstarch
- One cup of soy milk
- One tablespoon of cider vinegar
- Oil

Instructions:

1. Combine all spices in a shallow cup. Mix thoroughly.
2. Add half of the spice, corn starch, apple cider, soy milk and flour in a separate bowl and mix it thoroughly.
3. Over the cauliflower, pour the above mixture and combine well until they are covered.
4. Let it cool for 1 hour in a fridge.
5. Put a deep fry pan with oil over a moderate heat and let it for a while. Put pieces of cauliflower in oil and let it fry until it turns brown.
6. Serve with any sauce and garnishing of your liking.

❖ Mexican Stuffed Cheese Potatoes

Servings: 4
The period required: 35 minutes
Ingredients:

- Four potatoes
- 1 cup of black bean (rinsed)
- Vegetables of your liking (chopped)
- 1 cup of cheese (shredded)
- One tomato (chopped)
- Sour cream as garnishing (optional)

Instructions:

1. Put washed and peeled potatoes in the oven for 10 minutes and let it bake.
2. In meanwhile, chopped all vegetables and let it cook over moderate heat in a pan along with spices.
3. By using a knife, cut a shape of X on each baked potato. Use a fork or spoon to make a void in it.
4. Fill out that void with cooked mixture and sprinkle cheese over it. Let it heat for 4 minutes in an oven or until cheese is melted.
5. Garnish it with sour cream and serve.

❖ Tomato Cheese Toast

Servings: 2
Time took: 30 minutes

Ingredients:

- Four bread slices
- Four small pieces of cheese
- One tomato (finely chopped)
- Spices
- Olive Oil

Instructions:

1. Firstly, preheat the furnace to 200°C.
2. Grease the baking sheet well with oil.
3. Place bread slices in it and put over the cheese and other ingredients over it.
4. Bake until it mixes with the cheese.

❖ Guacamole Onion Rings

Servings: 6
Time took: 60 minutes

Ingredients:

- Three avocados (peeled and sliced)
- Lime zest
- One onion (finely sliced)
- Cilantro
- Garlic
- Salt and pepper as per your taste
- Flour for coating
- Two eggs (well beaten)
- 2 cups of panko bread crumbs

- Oil for frying

Instructions:

1. Mash the boiled avocados with lime juice in a mixing cup.
2. Combine all chopped vegetables and spices in a separate bowl.
3. Break the onion into chunks. Separate the layers cautiously into separate circles—lay-out onion rings on a tray.
4. Mix avocado mixture with each chunk of onion. Set it aside in the fridge.
5. In three distinct bowls, incorporate the flour, beating eggs, and panko breadcrumbs.
6. First, roll each one in flour, then eggs, then breadcrumbs. Coat the egg again and brush the breadcrumbs for the final time.
7. Place a pan with oil over moderate heat and fry those chunks with coating in it until it turns brown.
8. Sprinkle with lime juice and salt. Use sour cream to serve.

❖ Crusty Potato Fingers

Servings: 4
Time took: 40 minutes

Ingredients:

- 2 cups of boiled potatoes
- Half cup of semolina
- Salt, pepper and chilies as per your taste
- Coriander
- Warm water
- Oil for frying

Instructions:

1. Put half a cup of water and semolina together in a cup. Mix it well and set it aside.
2. Mix semolina mixture and boiled potatoes together.
3. Now, add all spices in it.
4. Mix it thoroughly and set it aside in a fridge.
5. Fry these in any shape of your liking in a frying pan over moderate flame for 4 minutes or until they turn brown.
6. In the above manner, cook all the potato fingers.
7. Serve with any sauce of your liking.

❖ Grilled Salsa Roja

Portions: 3 cups
Period Required: 30 minutes

Ingredients:

- Eight cherry tomatoes
- Half onion

- Four chiles
- Three cloves of garlic (minced)
- Salt, pepper and chilies as per your taste

Instructions:

1. Firstly, preheat the greased grill with medium flame.
2. Grill all vegetables over a preheated grill for about 5-8 minutes or until they are completely cooked.
3. Set them aside to cool down a bit.
4. In a blender, make a purée of the grilled vegetables and spices.
5. Serve with anything of your liking.

Chapter 04: Vegetarian Mexican Dinner Recipes

Dinner recipes are similar to lunch recipes because both are quite heavy. People usually either eat lunch heavy or dinner heavy. In this chapter, you will come to know about Vegetarian Mexican Dinner recipes. They are very lavish and full of flavors. Following are some amazing Mexican dinner recipes that you can make at home:

❖ Mexican Sheet Pan Supper

Servings: 3

Total time: 30 minutes

Ingredients:

- One sweet potato
- Two bell peppers (washed and sliced)
- One onion (finely sliced)
- One corn (drained)
- 1 cup of black beans (soaked and drained)
- Oil
- Spices
- For the topping: salsa

Instructions:

1. Cut sweet potatoes into cubes and let it boil in a pan filled with water for 13 minutes or until it turns tender.
2. You should preheat the oven up to 200C.
3. Grease a baking dish and put all ingredients and boiled sweet potatoes in it.
4. Let it bake for 20 minutes.

5. Serve it with a topping of salsa.

❖ Taco Soup

Servings: 7
Total time: 25 minutes
Ingredients:

- Oil
- ½ onion (finely sliced)
- Two cloves of garlic (minced properly)
- Salt, pepper, paprika, cumin and chilies as per your taste
- 1 cup of tomato (chopped or puree)
- 1 ½ cups of black beans (rinsed and soaked)
- One green chili (sliced)
- 2 cups of broth of vegetables
- 1 cup of corn
- 1 cup of cheese (shredded)

Instructions:

1. Put a pan with oil over moderate flame and let it heat for 2 minutes.
2. Add onions, garlic, spices and tomatoes. Let it cook for 10 minutes or until onions become translucent.
3. Add broth in it and put a lid over a pan and let it simmer for 15 minutes or until broth thickens.
4. For taste, add lime zest at the end.
5. Serve with garnishing of cheese.

❖ Roasted Cauliflower Street Tacos

Servings: 5
Time took: 40 minutes

Ingredients:

- 2 cups of cabbage (finely chopped)
- One tablespoon of apple cider vinegar
- One teaspoon of lime zest
- ½ tablespoon of honey (only for vegans)
- Salt and pepper as per your taste
- 2 cups of cauliflower (finely chopped)
- 1 cup of chickpeas (soaked and drained)
- Olive oil
- Salt, pepper, cumin and chili as per your taste
- Tortillas

For the sauce:

- One avocado
- One garlic (minced)
- Olive oil
- Lime zest
- Parsley
- Salt and pepper

Instructions:

1. Firstly, preheat the oven up to 200C.
2. Make slaw by mixing the ingredients above mentioned.
3. Then, make a sauce by blending all ingredients mentioned above.
4. Combine all the ingredients for Cauliflower Filling in a bowl. Place on a greased baking dish.
5. Let it bake for 25 minutes or until it turns brown.
6. Assemble all baked and mixed products over tortillas and serve.

❖ Soyrizo Potato Tacos

Servings: 10
Time took: 40 minutes

Ingredients:

- Two yellow potatoes (chopped)
- Olive oil
- Salt, pepper, chili, oregano and cumin as per your taste
- Ten ounces of soyrizo
- Ten tortillas
- Chopped lettuce for serving

Instructions:

1. In a broad bowl, place the cut potatoes and all spices in it. Mix it thoroughly.
2. Meanwhile, preheat the oven up to 220C.
3. Bake coated potatoes in the oven for 25 minutes or until it turns tender.
4. Then, you have to fry the potatoes for 4-5 minutes.
5. Prepare the soyrizo over a moderate flame in a pan for 5 minutes or until it is cooked perfectly.
6. Assemble potatoes first in each tortilla and put soyrizo mixture over it and then add your likeable topping over it.
7. Serve warm.

❖ Mexican Chili Rellenos

Servings: 6

Time took: 40 minutes

Ingredients:

- Six new chili peppers (sliced)
- 1 cup of Mexican cheese (strips)
- Chopped vegetables of your liking
- ½ tablespoon of baking powder
- 1 cup of flour
- The oil used for frying
- Eggs as per your requirement

Instructions:

1. Firstly, preheat the oven and place the oven rack in it.
2. Cover baking dish with foil and bake pepper in it for 10 minutes or until it turns blistered.
3. Let it set aside to cool. Peel the peppers under cold water and slice it to only get its long sides.
4. You have to sprinkle oil over it and fill it with cheese strips.
5. Lightly bake it to melt the cheese in it.
6. Meanwhile, whisk eggs and baking powder with the help of beater. Add flour in it.
7. Sauté the chopped vegetables in the pan over medium flame until the vegetables turn tender. Set it aside.
8. Put these vegetables in the pepper.
9. Cover all sides of pepper with a flour-egg mixture and fry it in frying pan until it turns brown and crisp.
10. Repeat this process for all peppers.
11. Serve it with your favorite sauce.

❖ Lentil Tacos

Servings: 2
Time took: 40 minutes

Ingredients:

- Olive oil
- One onion (finely sliced)
- Two teaspoons of garlic powder
- One cup of lentils (dried)
- One cup of vegetables (chopped)
- Salt, chili, paprika and pepper as per your taste
- Half cup of salsa (can be used as a topping)

Instructions:

1. Place a pan with two tablespoons of oil over a moderate flame and heat it for 3 minutes.
2. Place sliced onions in it and let it simmer for about 5 minutes or until onions begin to tender.
3. Add garlic, vegetable stock, spices and all other ingredients in it and let it cook for 30 minutes or until it turns tender.
4. When it is cooked, serve it with your favorite topping.

❖ Mashed Potato and Mashed Vegetable Enchilada

Serving: 5-6
Time took: 90 minutes

Ingredients:

- One broccoli (chopped into florets)
- 7 ounces of mushrooms

- 2 ½ zucchini (chopped)
- 1 ½ cups of carrots (chopped)
- Olive oil
- Salt and pepper as per your taste
- Water (2 or 3 cups)
- Milk (1 cup)
- Butter (half cup)
- Potato flakes (instant packet)
- 6 Tortillas
- 2 cups of enchilada sauce
- 2 cups of cheese (shredded)

Instructions:

1. Firstly, preheat the oven up to 200C.
2. Chop all vegetables as per instructions. Put them in greased baking dish. Sprinkle spices and oil over it. Bake for 30 minutes in an oven or until vegetables turns tender.
3. Add mashed potato flakes, milk, butter and water in a pot. Put a lid over the pot. Let it boil until it is cooked.
4. Sprinkle oil over tortillas. Reheat tortillas in a non-stick pan over moderate heat.
5. Assemble all cooked products in the middle of each tortilla. Spread sauce, spices and cheese over it. Roll it as you pleased.
6. Place tortillas in a baking dish and spread the remaining sauce and cheese over all tortillas evenly.
7. Bake it for 5-10 minutes or until cheese is properly melted.
8. Serve it.

❖ Sweet Potato Nachos

Servings: 6
Time took: 45 minutes

Ingredients:

- Three sweet potatoes (slice into circular shapes)
- Olive oil
- Salt, chili and pepper as per your taste
- ½ tablespoon of garlic powder
- ½ tablespoon of paprika powder
- ½ cup of black beans (soaked, rinsed and drained)
- ½ cup of cheese (shredded)
- ½ cup of tomatoes (chopped)
- Half cup of avocado (chopped)

Instructions:

1. Firstly, preheat the furnace up to 220C.
2. Place a foil over baking dish and grease it with oil.
3. Place sliced sweet potatoes in a baking dish. Sprinkle spices over it and let it bake for 10 minutes. Make sure to rotate the sides of sweet potato.
4. Add beans and cheese in the above baking dish. Let it bake for another 10 minutes or until beans turn soft.
5. Serve it with any sauce.

❖ Tofu Tacos with Chili

Servings: 7
Time took: 60 minutes
Ingredients:

- 16 ounces of tofu (pressed and dried)
- ¼ cup of soy sauce
- One tablespoon of lemon zest
- Vegan mayonnaise
- Salt, pepper and chilies as per your taste
- 1 cup of cabbage and avocado (chopped)
- Seven tortillas
- Half cup of scallions

Instructions:

1. Cut tofu into 1-inch cubes.
2. Sprinkle lime zest and soy sauce over the tofu and place it aside.
3. Fry the chopped vegetables in a pan over moderate flame.
4. Meanwhile, coat tofu with corn starch and mix it in the above pan. Cook it until it turns brown, and vegetables turn tender.
5. Reheat the tortillas on the skillet.
6. Assemble the cooked mixture along with sauce over the tortillas.
7. Serve it with any topping.

❖ Jalapeno Chickpea Mac and Cheese Pasta

Servings: 8

Time took: 45 minutes

Ingredients:

- 17 ounces of chickpea and lentil pasta
- 2 ½ jalapenos (chopped without seeds)
- 1 cup of chickpea (rinsed and drained)
- Salt, paprika, chili, cumin and pepper as per your taste

- Garlic powder
- Olive oil
- ¼ cup of milk
- ¼ cup of broth (vegetables)
- ½ tablespoon of yeast
- Two tablespoons of flour

Instructions:

1. Preheat the furnace up to 220C. Fill a big pot with 6 cups of water and put a lid over it and bring it to a boil.
2. Mix chickpeas with spices. Spread and bake on a baking sheet for 18 minutes or until it turns tender.
3. Boil pasta in the above boiling water as per given instruction behind the package. Drain it well.
4. Sprinkle spices over pasta and place it in a baking dish. Let it bake for 3 minutes.
5. Meanwhile, blend coconut milk, broth, yeast and flour in another deep saucepan. Let it cook until it thickened. When the sauce is prepared, let it put aside.
6. Mix the pasta, chickpea with the sauce.
7. Garnish and serve with cilantro.

❖ Sofritas Tofu Burrito

Servings: 8
Time took: 60 minutes

Ingredients:

- One block tofu (dried properly and cut into cubes)
- Olive oil
- One cup of each red and green pepper (diced)
- One cup of onion (diced)
- Salt, pepper, chili and cumin as per your taste
- One tablespoon of tomato puree
- 1 cup of tomatoes (roasted and chopped)
- Half cup of broth (vegetable)

Instructions:

1. Firstly, preheat the oven up to 220C. Grease a baking dish.
2. Place cubes of tofu in the baking dish and sprinkle oil over it. Bake it for 10 minutes or more. Then, set it aside.
3. For the preparation of sofritas, sauté all the vegetables and spices in a deep pan.
4. Add baked tofu, broth and spices (if you want to) in the above deep pan. Put a lid on it and boil it for 15 minutes over low flame.
5. Thicken the consistency of mixture as per your liking.
6. Add lime zest over it and serve in a dish.

❖ Spinach Tortillas

Servings: 6
Period Required: 25 minutes
Ingredients:

- Flour (2 cups)
- Cooked spinach (1 cup)
- Water
- Salt and pepper as per your taste

Instructions:

1. Firstly, cook spinach as per your liking.
2. Blend the cooked spinach, and you can also add spices in it as per your taste.
3. Knead dough by mixing spinach puree, water and salt.
4. Dust the flour on a board and cut the dough into around 6-8 pieces. Roll the portions into balls with your hands to use.
5. Make tortillas by using these dough balls.
6. Cook tortillas in a skillet over a high flame. You can also add oil to it.
7. Carefully cook tortilla from both sides.
8. Repeat the process.
9. Serve all tortillas with a sauce of your liking.

❖ Mexican Pasta Salad

Servings: 6

Period Required: 25 minutes

Ingredients:

- One packet of pasta
- 1 cup of corn (drained)
- One can of black beans (soaked and drained)
- Olive oil
- One onion and bell pepper (chopped)
- ½ tomato (sliced)
- Cilantro
- 1 cup of cheese (shredded)

Ingredients for Dressing:

- Olive oil
- Fresh juice of a lime
- Two tablespoons of garlic
- One teaspoon of honey
- Half teaspoon of cumin
- Half teaspoon of paprika
- Salt
- Pepper

Instructions:

1. Cook the pasta according to the box instructions.
2. Combine the cooled spaghetti, rice, beans, olives, bell pepper, tomatoes and red onion in a wide dish.
3. Mix above ingredients of dressing to prepare a dressing for this recipe.
4. Put it over the pasta mixture. Mix it thoroughly.
5. Toss cilantro on the top of it.
6. Cover with the cheese and serve it.

❖ Tomatillo Poblano White Beans

Servings: 6

Total time: 40 minutes

Ingredients:

- 2 cups Tomatillos diced
- 1 cup poblano (sliced)
- 1 cup of onion (chopped)
- One jalapeno (sliced and without seeds)
- Salt and pepper as per your taste
- ½ teaspoon of cumin
- 1 cup of dried and soaked beans

- 1 cup of water or more
- One tablespoon of oregano

Instructions:

1. Blend all vegetables together. Blend until the veggies are thin, but not purified.
2. Over the moderate fire, pour the blended veggies in a deep pan. Add spices in it and let it cook for a while.
3. Add the beans, water and oregano to the above mixture and swirl to mix it. Put on the cover and let it boil over low heat for 30 minutes.
4. Prior to serving, apply salt and pepper to taste.

❖ Casserole and Cheese

Cooking Time: 35 minutes
Serving: 9

Ingredients:

- Salt and pepper, to taste
- Sour cream, as required
- Onion, one
- Minced garlic, three
- Mixed cheese, one cup
- Avocado, one
- Jalapeno, one
- Taco seasoning, one teaspoon
- Tortillas, nine
- Tomatoes, one
- Mix vegetables, half cup
- Vegetable oil, two teaspoons
- Cilantro, as required

Instructions:

1. Add the vegetable oil and cook the onions in a pan.
2. Add the minced garlic and cook.
3. Cook well and add tomatoes, taco seasoning, salt, and pepper into the mixture.
4. Add the mix vegetables and cook for two minutes.
5. Transfer the mixture into a baking dish and top with cheese blend.
6. Bake it for five minutes.
7. Add the cilantro on top and serve it with tortillas and desired toppings.

❖ Spicy Vegan Tofu Enchilada

Servings: 5-6
Time took: 40 minutes

Ingredients:

- Six light taco shells or tortillas
- One pack of tofu (dried and cut into cubes)
- Olive oil
- Two teaspoons of seasoning of taco
- Diced tomatoes
- 1 cup of black beans (rinsed and soaked)
- One diced onion

Instructions:

1. Firstly, preheat the oven up to 220C.
2. Dry out tofu completely. Cut into cubes.
3. Sprinkle seasoning over tofu. Place it in a skillet with oil over moderate flame and cook until it turns brown.

4. Mix the peas, black beans and onion in a bowl and put aside meanwhile the tofu is frying.
5. Mix together the sauce and chipotle seasoning in a different bowl and set aside. Take half cup of the sauce and dump it into a greased baking dish to scatter the sauce out over the dish.
6. To prepare the enchiladas: dump into one tortilla a tablespoon of the tomato mixture, then place a tablespoon of the fried tofu. Fold the tortilla and bring the part of the fold down into the baking dish. Repeat this step until all the enchiladas are completed.
7. Add the remaining mixture sauce over the enchiladas and let it bake for 17 minutes.
8. Serve it.

❖ Crockpot Quinoa Tacos

Servings: 5

Time took: 30 minutes

Ingredients:

- 1 of a cup of quinoa
- ½ cup of vegetable broth
- 1 cup of beans
- One diced tomatoes
- Taco seasoning

Instructions:

1. In a stockpot, combine all ingredients together.
2. Add taco seasoning in it.
3. Cook for three hours, on high temperature.
4. Serve it with tortillas.

❖ Colorful Vegetable Fajitas

Servings: 4
Time took: 40 minutes
Ingredients:

- Eight tortillas of flour
- Vegetable oil
- One red onion
- One green bell pepper (chopped)
- One red bell pepper (chopped)
- One teaspoon of garlic (minced)
- Salsa
- Salt and pepper as per your taste
- ½ tablespoon of cilantro

Instructions:

1. Firstly, preheat oven at 220C. Grease baking dish.
2. Place the tortillas in the oven. Bake until fully cooked.
3. Heat oil over a moderate flame in a pan. Add all spices and ingredients in it except veggies. Let it cook for 5-10 minutes.
4. Stir in the veggies with the squash. Cover, then let it simmer for more five minutes.
5. Sprinkle with cheese and cilantro and spoon the vegetable mixture equally down the centers of the soft tortillas. Roll up some tortillas, then serve.

❖ Asparagus and Cheese Quesadillas

Serving: 5
Time taken: 35 minutes
Ingredients:

- Olive oil
- Half pound of asparagus (chopped)
- Salt and pepper
- 2 tortillas of flour
- 4 ounces of cheese
- ½ cup of new cilantro (chopped)

Instructions:

1. In a pan over moderate flame, heat olive oil and cook the asparagus, swirling periodically, until it turns soft. Turn off the heat and season with spices.
2. Spread cheese over one surface of each tortilla. On each tortilla, position the asparagus and cilantro and roll half the tortillas over the ingredients to create quesadillas.
3. Over moderate flame, put the quesadillas in a pan and cook for 5 minutes on each hand, or until it is lightly browned.
4. Garnish with according to your taste and choice.

Conclusion

Mexican cooking is incredibly vast and amazing. It started from Mexico yet got popular enough to spread worldwide, and it is being eaten everywhere on the planet. The individuals of the United States of America love Mexican food, and they devour it on a daily basis.

Mexicans food is basically related to carnivorous eating, but with the time, Mexicans are embracing vegetarian and vegan diets too. If you study more about Mexican cuisines then, you will find out that vegetarian Mexican cuisines are way lesser than non-vegetarian cuisines. Mexico is mostly about citrus fruits, varieties of legumes, a broad selection of spices, and a preference for new cooking ingredients. It is a meat-focused country, and vegetarianism is not popular, however, luckily, there are vegetarian ingredients in many dishes, such as corn tortillas, rice, cheese, and vegetables.

Enchilada, Quesadilla, Burritos, Meatless Lasagna, Pies, Vegan burgers, Tortillas and much more are the best options for vegetarians in Mexico. At street stalls, these fast and inexpensive snacks can be found. Most of these are based on corn tortillas, and you can typically get vegetarian versions and then liven them up with typical toppings such as salsas, even though it is only cheese. In this book, we have given 77 distinct recipes of Vegetarian Mexican cuisine that include assorted dishes that you would love.

The given recipes incorporate solid breakfast, lunch, snacks and dinner. Most importantly, these recipes are all vegetarian in nature. An individual who does not normally cook, for the most part, can undoubtedly make every one of these recipes with the definite fixing rundown and simple to adhere directions that are referenced with every recipe in the book. After reading this book, you will be able to make delicious Vegetarian Mexican recipes at home.

CPSIA information can be obtained
at www.ICGtesting.com
Printed in the USA
LVHW011633230621
690870LV00013BB/823

9 781802 764123